SALES FUNNEL GROWTH

"Discover The Secrets To Creating A Sales Funnel That Will Grow Your Business"

By: Tom Kustra

Disclaimer

This e-book has been written for information purposes only. Every effort has been made to make this e-book as complete and accurate as possible. However, there may be mistakes in typography or content. Also, this e-book provides information only up to the publishing date. Therefore, this e-book should be used as a guide - not as the ultimate source.

The purpose of this e-book is to educate. The author and the publisher does not warrant that the information contained in this e-book is fully complete and shall not be responsible for any errors or omissions. The author and publisher shall have neither liability nor responsibility to any person or entity with respect to any loss or damage caused or alleged to be caused directly or indirectly by this e-book.

About the Author

Tom Kustra is an entrepreneur living in Toronto who loves sharing knowledge and helping others on the topics of web design, inbound marketing, entrepreneurship and technology.

Tom is a passionate person who will go the extra mile and over-deliver.

Tom's words of wisdom:

"The world's biggest problems are the biggest business opportunities. In order to succeed in an ever changing world, you MUST adapt, learn, and grow with technology, not against it."

If you would like to learn more from Tom Kustra please visit:

www.TomKusta.com

www.MiticoMedia.com

Table of Contents

Introduction

No matter what it is you're trying to sell on the web, a sales funnel is the number one way to do it. This is the most systematic way to build trust, to build a relationship and to encourage people to want your brand before making a sale – and it is incredibly powerful when done well.

Take a look around the web and chances are that you'll have come across a large number of sales funnels without even realizing it. So what exactly is a sales funnel? How does it work? And how can you tap into its power for yourself?

Those are the questions we're going to be asking and *answering* in this e-book. By the end, you'll know exactly what a funnel is and why it's so important. Moreover, you'll be able to build your own sales funnel from scratch and use it to capture leads and convert them into paying customers.

Once you understand the science behind this, you'll see why it's the most effective way to build profits and you'll be able to turn any product or service into a massive success.

What is a Sales Funnel?

Before we go any further, it would perhaps be useful to explain exactly what a sales funnel is and what you'll be using it for.

In essence, a sales funnel can be imagined like a funnel for customers. You start out with a broad opening to capture as many leads as possible and then you gradually narrow those leads down to only the most engaged and interested customers so that you can sell to them. All the while, you'll be building trust, building engagement and priming them to make a purchase.

You can also think about this as a ladder, which each rung taking your customers closer to the top where you'll eventually try to sell to them.

In practice, what this means is a series of different marketing strategies, each arranged in such a way as to build more and more targeted leads for your business. So you might start with a simple advert, or a blog post and then move on to an email list, then a 'free report', then a seminar, then a small product sale and then a *big* sale.

Each of these marketing stages is a rung on a ladder. It's a little further down the funnel. And each time a customer clicks on the next link, or follows you to the next step, they are becoming more and more likely to buy from you.

As mentioned, there's a good chance you'll have encountered different sales funnels in your travel around the web: you may even have bought products from others through this method. You might have come across a blog and signed up to the mailing list for instance, and then been told to click on the link therein in order to see a free seminar. And then maybe the free seminar asked you to sign up for the *next* seminar which would cost a "little bit of money"

And you may have come across it on YouTube too. For example, Tai Lopez is something of a flashy business man who is willing to use everything at his disposal to capture new leads and sales.

He employs a sales funnel *very* well. If you go on YouTube to watch a video, his ad will very often show up.

So even if you want to have a job, you want to diversify.

13:05 / 13:40

The guy then goes on to talk about his cars or his massive house and this makes you want to watch – even if only because it annoys you.

At the end of the video, he offers to show you how to get his three most important tips for making money. And because it's free, why *wouldn't* you click it? Only at this point, you're becoming more and more involved with his brand and more and more likely to become a paying customer. When you watch this 'free' video, which is on his site or channel, you'll then be told you can get even more information by signing up for a free report. In fact, this report is *key* to understanding the video. If you do this, then Tai now has your details *and* the confirmation that you're interested in what he has to sell!

You've gone from a 'cold lead' (someone on YouTube, targeted based on your video watching choices), to a 'warm lead' (someone who has demonstrated an interest) to eventually a 'qualified lead'.

The way Tai does this is a little transparent and a little cynical – but it's how *all* the big names operate including the likes of Tony Robbins, Tim Ferriss and Pat Flynn. And it's exactly what you should be doing if you want to make sales. Note that this doesn't mean you have to impress people with exotic cars and mansions like Tai! Just that you need to think about your marketing strategy in steps and stages and understand the psychology of the way you're dealing with people.

What You Will Learn

Reading this book, you'll learn precisely how to employ these kinds of techniques yourself and we're going to break down all the different tools, resources and tips you need to execute this plan perfectly. What's more though, is that we're also going to look at some higher level concepts.

You'll learn how to sell anything, how to write persuasive copy that people simply can't ignore and how to build a massive following so that you don't just have visitors and customers – you have loyal fans!

Specifically, you'll discover:

- Why sales funnels are THE most effective tool for sales

- All the tools and resources you need to construct the ultimate sales funnel

- How to target your audience and bring the right people to the first stage of your funnel

- How to use persuasive writing to convince people to buy anything

- How to engage your audience and build trust and real following

- How to maximize conversion rates

- How to make people buy from you more than once

- How to utilize an understanding of psychology to skyrocket your sales

- What the different options are for your sales funnels

- How to stand out and be different

- And much more!

Chapter 1: Why Sales Funnels? Understanding the 5 Touches

Imagine if someone came up to you in the street and asked you if you'd like to buy a $5,000 watch.

99.9999% of the time, you would say no to that offer.

Why? Well, apart from the fact that you might not want a watch (you are a 'cold lead' in that respect), there's also the small issue of trust, recognition and authority. You don't know who this person is, you've been given no reason to trust them and you're probably *not* going to want to hand over any cash.

That's why companies don't do this. Instead, they give you fliers. Fliers are things you can choose to accept or throw away – but either way, they don't cost you anything and you won't feel that you're being pressured into anything.

Other stores do something different: they give away freebies. Walk past Starbucks and you'll often find them giving away free samples of their new drinks and cakes for you to try. Again, you can easily walk away if you're not interested and you won't feel you're being strong-armed. If you like the free sample though, then you can come in and try whatever else they're offering.

If you try and sell to people right away on your website though, then you're the equivalent of someone trying to sell thousand dollar watches in the street. And if that's the only thing you're offering and the only way that your visitors can engage with you, then they're just going to say 'no thanks' and leave, giving you no way to contact them again and no way to get them back. As you might have guessed, this is a poor strategy!

Try to imagine it from their perspective: they have typed 'fitness tips' into Google, found your page essentially by accident and now you're trying to sell them your training program for $500. People do not make decisions on that basis unless they're *loaded* with cash. They'll see you're trying to sell them, write you off as spam and then *leave*.

The Alternative

Now imagine the alternative: the sales funnel technique.

They do the same thing: they type in 'fitness tips' and they land on your site where they get some great information *right away*. That information is unique, interesting and useful but at the bottom, it tells the audience that if they want more great tips – your '5 Most Powerful Tips' – then all they have to do is to enter their details to receive your free report.

There's very little reason for them not to do this: you have demonstrated that you're able to provide value and you're offering something for free. The only price they pay is to allow you to contact them in future – but as you will point out, they can always just unsubscribe if they don't want to hear anything more from you.

They get their free report and once again, they find it is really good. At the same time though, they're now getting emails from you – emails with highly engaging and interesting subject lines. The people who click those emails are now showing very good engagement and you can see that they're the kinds of people that might be willing to buy from you.

Those people will receive an email on an automated basis that invites them to an exciting free conference where they can here you talk online about fitness. This is a great, rare opportunity and if they like what you've done so far, they should *definitely* get involved.

They do that and because they've gone so far out of their way to hear you and they've listened to the whole thing, they've now made the full transition to *fan*. They are now *engaging* with you in a big way and going out of their way to hear more from you. This makes a massive difference because in their *own mind,* it will inform them that you are someone they're interested in hearing more from.

Quick Psychology Lesson!

This relates to an interesting aspect of psychology called 'cognitive dissonance'. Did you know that the best way to make someone like you is to get them to do things for you? Why? Because this creates a state of cognitive dissonance in their mind otherwise. The brain like congruence – it likes to see that your actions are consistent with your beliefs.

If you do something for someone that takes a lot of effort then, the brain assumes that you *must* really like them to have been willing to go to such lengths.

The same thing works here. If someone engages with your brand – if they rush to your seminar and wait for you to come online – they tell themselves that they *must* be big fans of your work!

At the same time, when someone has put a lot of effort into something, that then creates a strong motivation to 'get something from it'. Your audience will want closure and the best way to do that is by buying from you!

After your free seminar, the next stage is to sell to them. This is them taking the next step and transitioning from a visitor or a fan into a paying customer. This is the point where they become willing to buy from you and where you can start making money.

BUT it's not going to be the 'big ticket' item yet. Instead, you're just going to sell them something very small. This very small thing is going to be something along the lines of an eBook, or a short course. It should cost anywhere from $5 to $50 but what it's doing is demonstrating that they can buy from you and trust you.

Why Your Small Sale is So Important

This 'small sale' is a super important point to include in a sales funnel (and one that not everyone will know to include). The basic idea behind this, you're giving your audience the chance to buy from you without too much risk.

Because, as we saw with our watch salesman, one of the biggest 'barriers to sale' is risk. People are naturally risk averse and they hate the idea that they might hand over their cash, only for you to go running off into the sunset laughing at their stupidity. They need to see that they can buy from you and trust you.

And if they don't know that, then getting them to spend $5,000 is going to be very hard. But now sell them something for $5 and you can get them to say 'why not'? They've seen you can offer value from the other steps in your sales funnel and the risk of losing $5 is not too serious. So they take their chance. Only now, they know they can trust you, they know that you're able to deliver value and their details will already be saved in your payment system.

That means that to make the big purchase, you only have to persuade them that your product is worth it and get them to take the plunge with *one click*. This is MUCH easier than trying to get them to take the plunge when they've never dealt with you before.

And finally, it's off the back of that sale that you're going to then sell your big ticket item. They've heard all your free content, they've read your e-book… but if they want to get the *very most* from you and if they want to see the very best, most powerful tips for their training, then they need to upgrade to your most expensive offer.

Alternatively, you might make multiple sales of products that increase in value gradually over time and that way each increase in cost will seem very small. This way, you are making 'incremental' increases in price and thus people will gradually increase the value that they're spending with you and become increasingly likely to make the transition to the truly 'big ticket' items. See the chapter on pricing and 'moving the free line' for more on this.

But in short, *that* is how you sell a $5,000 product.

One More Important Point

One more important point is to understand and utilize the power of social influence and membership. This is one more tool you're going to use to get people to really want to take the next step down your sales funnel – the idea of belonging to something and being a part of something and the idea of being 'left out' unless they take that step. So you're going to point out to your audience that buying your big ticket item means being a part of your movement, means getting the *full* experience and means seeing the VIP content that your 'regular' customers don't get to see. They'll be part of an elite community and they'll get access to top secret information!

The Five Touches

Hopefully you now understand how a sales funnel works and why it's such an important tool for maximizing your sales. At the same time though, it's worth noting that the steps themselves don't need to look like this. You might not have a mailing list, you might not have a seminar – but you can still create a funnel.

What's important, is simply that you have a series of escalating 'steps', with each one increasing engagement and building your fan base further.

So the question now becomes: how many steps constitute a 'funnel'? While this varies from case to case, the best answer is five. That's because research tells us that it takes *five touches* to sell to someone. This means they should interact with your business at least five times before you try and shift your big ticket item. This is enough to take someone from being completely unaware of your brand, to being familiar enough with you that they are willing to put their money and their trust in your products.

Chapter 2: What Constitutes a Sales Funnel?

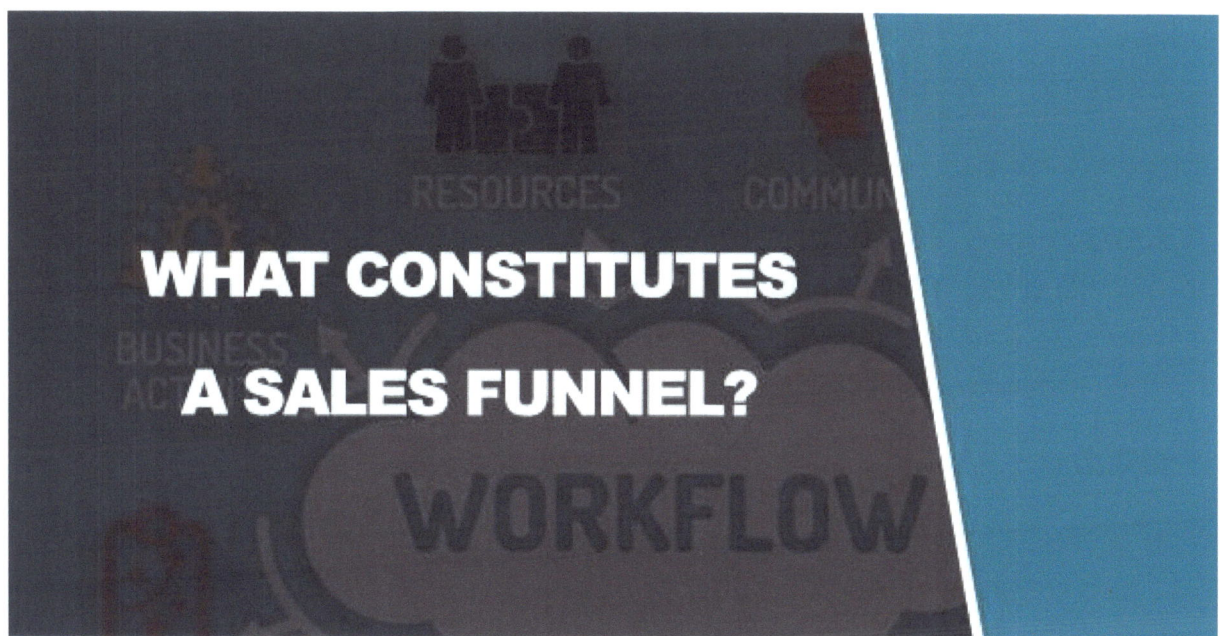

In that last chapter, we looked at an example of a typical sales funnel and how it might work. We saw that you should utilize five unique steps but that these steps could vary depending on your business and your preference.

So now the question is: what options do you have for your steps? What kinds of touches can you employ to get the max amount of customers?

Here are some potential 'touches' you can use to bring your customers in and to establish that all important *trust and familiarity* before you sell to them:

The First Touch

Blog

The most obvious first touch that a lot of sites and businesses will use is the blog. This is a great place to provide some free value, to demonstrate your knowledge and authority and to provide tips and advice. Your blog should include free information and articles relating to your business/niche and you should work to make sure these are well thought-out, well written and provide tons of value. The more unique, useful and insightful information you offer here, the more people are going to trust you and believe that you can offer the value that they're looking for and that is going to be worth them paying for!

Squeeze Page

A squeeze page is a page that is *all about* trying to get people to subscribe to a mailing list. You can drive people here using PPC and other forms of advertising and then simply set out an excellent case for them to subscribe to you. It can work alongside a blog or it can work on its own.

YouTube

You can use YouTube as an excellent place to have your first touch. Here, you can create a video you know people will search for and attempt to offer some real value, or you can create a video like the one Tai Lopez uses that we discussed earlier. The great thing about a video is that it is so engaging and will be so effective at grabbing attention, holding it and allowing you to convey your points to an audience that is listening.

Guest Post

There's no reason that your first touch needs to be on your own site. If you write a guest post for another big channel, then you can get their fans and followers to find your content and you can then bring those viewers and readers over to your own channels.

The Second Touch

Mailing List

A mailing list is a great second touch and one that the vast majority of brands will use. Email still has a great level of conversion and open-rate and this is due to the fact that it is so personal and direct. It also means you're not relying on a third party (like Google or Facebook) and it allows you to address your audience directly.

Social Media

The next best thing to a mailing list is social media. If you can get someone to like you on Facebook, or to follow you on Twitter, then you are giving yourself the opportunity to contact them in future. And like subscribers, people who follow you on social media are taking that psychological step that makes them 'fans'.

You can also try alternative options for your social media too. SnapChat for example has a surprisingly high engagement!

Forum, Comments Section

Inviting people to take part in a community is a brilliant way to get them excited for your brand and committed to the idea. Once people start having conversations in a group with your name on it, they will feel like they 'belong' and it will be very hard for them to turn off from your brand and to break their engagement.

YouTube

The YouTube equivalent of this is to get someone to subscribe to your channel. When they do this, they'll then see new videos as you post them and this is an excellent way to get them to see your new content and to reach them with new promotions and offers.

The Third Touch

Free Report

The third touch should be something that requires them to take another action and it should be something a bit lengthier that forces them to engage with your content. A free report is a great example of this and it's a good chance for you to demonstrate the value you're capable of delivering.

Video Seminar

Video seminars are great because they are live events. This means people will need to prepare to listen to them and will hopefully be looking forward to the event as they anticipate it. Making people wait for something is a perfect way to get them to want it more! What's more, a live video seminar is something that people will feel very engaged with and that will give them a very direct interaction with you – it's like they're able to talk to you in person!

Free Chat

Similar, is to offer some kind of free chat or consultation. Going back to our example of selling a training program for instance, you could offer a free 'fitness consult' and recommend some exercises, diet plans etc. to your audience.

This can be one-to-one if you're willing to put the time in (it's a fantastic way to build true fans, which we will discuss in the next chapter! Another option though is to have a group chat, such as one on Google Hangouts. Want to make this even more exciting? Make it invite only!

The Fourth Touch

E-book

Your fourth touch is going to be the small sale that will help to engage your audience. Ideally, this will be something that will offer a *similar* service/value to the main product that you're trying to shift and that way it should be able to demonstrate that the thing you are in fact selling for more is going to be worth more money.

Super Cheap Items

Or, if your only interest is getting people to buy from you and demonstrating your trustworthiness, then you can always just sell something incredibly cheaply. This might mean something as simple as selling a phone case or a t-shirt – perhaps just for a couple of dollars.

Selling Lots of Items of Increasing Value

Many a sales funnel will be *built* around just sales. The sales funnel we've described so far is one with a low 'free line' (this is discussed in more detail in a subsequent chapter). The more you give away for free, the better.

But it's also possible to put multiple purchases below the free line. Rather than selling one item, then your big ticket item, you can instead go through gradually more expensive products and build this up to the point where your customer eventually pays for something very expensive.

This is the best way to get people to buy the very highest ticket items. This way, they will be making multiple purchases that increase in value and thereby each step will seem slightly smaller. This way, it won't seem like such a big deal to eventually spend that much money. The steps are incremental and thus they *seem* smaller and more palatable.

Free Trial

If you are selling SAAS (Software as a Service) or similar, then another good option is to offer a free trial of whatever it is that you're going to sell. A free trial is much easier to convince someone to try than actually selling to them; if you handle this correctly, they'll still be handing over their details and they might even input their card details so that you can charge them should they fail to cancel their membership after the first month.

T-shirts and Gifts

Another alternative to actually selling is to give something away for free. One of the best examples of doing this is to give away a free 'promotional gift'. These are things that have your branding on them and might include the likes of t-shirts or mugs.

These are very cheap to produce, which makes them ideal as 'loss leaders'. What's more though, is that you can include your branding and that way get free marketing and exposure every time your fans use those items. At the same time, by wearing a t-shirt with your brand on it, your visitors will feel much more engaged and committed to your brand, to the point where they might want to demonstrate their allegiance in other ways!

The Final Touch

It should go without saying that your final touch is going to be your actual sale. This is what everything up to this point has been leading up to and when your visitors arrive on your site, they should hopefully be engaged, committed and ready to buy from you.

All that remains is for you to make that final push to convert them into a customer – and you might do that with a series of emails, or you might do it with an effective 'sales page'.

In chapter 4, you'll learn how to use persuasive sales copy to convince people to buy anything. You can use these techniques to convert those fans into paying customers but also to help with every other stage of your funnel!

First, let's take a look at some of the more advanced techniques you can use for creating your sales funnel!

Chapter 3: Advanced Techniques – Live Video Streaming and More

There are a number of more advanced techniques and strategies you can add into this mix however, many of which will help you to engage your audience even more, or in an entirely different way.

Newer and More Interesting Steps

For example, one step that people often won't use is to offer a free *app* download. This works well because people will often get excited by the prospect of getting an app – they can see this as an exciting free product rather than something dull like a mailing list. This then gives you a very slick and polished way to reach your audience though, or for them to check in with you. It also means you can use 'push notifications' to sell products!

Another example of a more advanced 'touch' you can use, is to try live video streaming. Right now, live streaming is all the rage. Effectively, this means using a tool like Periscope, Meerkat or Facebook in order to stream a recording of yourself live to your visitors and followers. When done correctly, this will allow you to engage a large audience of followers and they will in turn be able to respond to what you're saying, to like comments and to ask questions.

Live streaming is taking off in a big way at the moment. It's a great way to find new potential customers because the various channels are currently so quiet that *any* video here will quickly and easily be found by people searching for new things to watch.

What's more, is that live streaming allows you to interact *directly* with your audience. People will be able to watch you as though they were in the room with you and can ask questions that you will be able to respond to directly. This builds much more trust and makes them feel as though they know you already – this can help a great deal when it comes to sales. And it sure doesn't hurt that live streaming makes you look very modern and 'on the ball' at the same time! This is a cool and interesting alternative to having an online seminar with something like U-Conference.

Targeting Your Audience and Finding Leads

One of the most important considerations when building a sales funnel, is how you're going to get people to the start of that funnel in the first place. What's more, is asking how you're going to get the *right* people to the start of that funnel. This is where something called 'targeting' comes in.

Going back to our example of the shady watch salesman, one of the biggest problems he had (other than the trust issue), was that he doesn't know who we are. We have shown no interest in watches and for all he knows, we might hate wearing things on our wrist. Or perhaps we've just been given a beautiful new watch and only feel the need for one. For this reason alone, our watch guy is not likely to have much luck.

But now imagine that he is using targeting to sell only to people with a high chance of being interested. One way he could do this is to stand outside the 'Watch Lovers' Convention'. Another option would be to visit people's homes who have answered a survey saying they're in the market for a watch.

Shady watch guy is still doing a lot of stuff wrong but simply by approaching that right audience, he's going to see a BIG improvement in his conversion rates.

And that's what we need to do too – bring the right people to our site to begin with. And to do that, we need to first identify who our buyer is. This means working out who our 'buyer persona' is.

Buyer Persona

A buyer persona is a fictional biography of the 'ideal customer' for your product. This means that they're the exact sort of person liable to want to buy from you.

In profiling this person though, you're not just going to be looking at the demographics. Demographics are things like the buyer age, sex, location and marital status. This is important but you want to go deeper by thinking about their philosophies, their politics, their other interests and more. Once you've created your imaginary biography, this will then allow you to market your product in the very places where this person is most likely to be. That might mean finding forums that discuss the *other* subjects they're interested in, or it might mean finding blogs with a similar central concept to write guest posts for.

This will essentially allow you to find a good 'route to market', which is anywhere that your ideal buyer persona is likely to spend time as a captive audience member. A brilliant example might be a magazine on a particular subject.

If you can find your route to market and you can match that market with the right product and sales funnel, then you will be almost guaranteed to see success for your products.

Chapter 4: Persuasive Writing and How to Use AIDA in Your Marketing

No matter how good your sales funnel though, it will only be as strong as your weakest link.

And in many cases, that weakest link is the fifth and final touch: the point where you actually come to sell your product. A lot of people just don't know how to make their items sell and they don't know how to make something seem really exciting and necessary.

This is where persuasive writing comes in and it's where 'AIDA' comes in. Read on and learn how to sell anything to anyone…

What is AIDA?

AIDA is a concept that can help make it that little bit easier for you to sell your products and make money online. The general idea here is that you need to take your visitors from the point where they've never heard of you, to the point where they're ready to buy. Sound familiar?

Only this time, we're focusing more on the specific product rather than on the brand more generally. To that end, AIDA stands for:

Awareness

Interest

Desire

Action

You can't make someone interested in your product until they're aware of it. You can make them want it until they've learned about it. And you can encourage them to click buy until you've made them really *want* what you're offering.

This AIDA structure is a highly useful guide! You can even build AIDA into each touch then, by starting by teasing your product and then building on that by providing more and more information and generally making it sound more desirable.

Either that, or you can place awareness in your second stage and then provide the interest and desire in the next two. You can even place all five steps in the final touch through your sales page – depending on what it is that you're trying to sell and your broader strategy.

However you approach it though, in order to sell the idea, you're going to need to be able to use the right persuasive writing. Which is where our next step comes in…

How to Use Persuasive Writing

At some point, you're going to need to build interest and desire for your product. How do you do that? How can you make someone want what you have?

Grabbing Attention

Well, it all starts with attention and engagement – which are increasingly difficult things to accomplish in today's world. These days, everyone is in a rush, everyone is always buys and it's increasingly rare to get a chance to just sit down and read a long piece of text. Studies even suggest that the internet and technology in general is causing symptoms very similar to ADD in a lot of people!

So your first objective is to get people to stop and pay attention. That means you need to write in a manner that is efficient and to the point. Avoid long winded sentences or flamboyant language – aim to get your point across in as few words as possible.

Another tip is to try writing with a narrative structure. In other words, make your sales pitch into a story! One of the most common and popular ways to do this is to write the story of how your product helped you – this works wonders because people find it hard to turn off from stories – we always want to know how they end and we want to learn as much as we can about them. This is why we'll often stay up all night watching trashy TV!

You can also grab attention right away by using a controversial or shocking opening sentence that will increase interest and engagement and make it hard for people to just turn off.

Another tip is to make sure people don't just leave without reading everything is to try and write in a way that makes it easy to skim through quickly.

If you take a look at most sales pages, you'll notice that they're very long and narrow, that they utilize lots of long, detailed headers and that they have lots of bold, underlined or red text.

The idea here is that most people will skim through your content anyway – so you need to ensure that they can do so and still get the *whole* story. Even just the headlines alone should give enough information that someone might be interested to buy, while the bold and underlined words will also jump out and grab attention.

This way **<u>even if people are in a hurry</u>**, they're still going to be ENGAGED and hopefully **buy your product**!!

Selling the Dream

So now they're reading, what are you going to do with that hard-won attention? The answer is that you need to sell the dream and sell your 'value proposition'. You need to get people dreaming about your product and truly wishing they owned it.

This is something we'll talk about more in subsequent chapters but ultimately, the objective is to make sure people think of your product in emotional terms. They need to understand how your product can make their lives better and why they really need it.

What is a value proposition? Essentially, it means understanding how your product really makes lives better. What is the real *value* in your product? *Why* will people buy it? People don't buy a fitness e-book for a good read. They don't even buy a fitness book to get fitter. They buy fitness books to feel good about themselves, to impress women or men, to have confidence and good health. That's the 'dream' and that's the emotion you need to tap into.

If your product is about making money, then the dream is power, influence and the resources to avoid the stress of debt, to go on big holidays and to own a big beautiful house!

Of course you also need to describe the product itself and precisely what it entails – it can't all just be abstract.

Building Trust and Authority

The next thing you need to do is to build trust and authority. You're selling this dream and showing exactly how you're going to help people get there. But that's not enough on its own because people need to trust you.

This is partly what your sales funnel has been all about leading up to this. But you can also further enhance this effect during your sales pitch. You can help people to trust you *and* remove risk by:

- Using social proof like reviews and testimonials

- Using money back guarantees and other safety measures that make the buyer feel safe

- Appealing to stats and statistics – such as studies that backup your claims

- Appealing to figures of authority and thought leaders in your niche

- Providing your own credentials

Do all this and you'll find people are more likely to take that risk and buy from you.

Removing Barriers to Sale

Finally, you need to remove those barriers to sale. One way to do this is by combating the dreaded 'buyers' remorse'. This is the sense of guilt that people can feel after they've bought something. You need to remove this by demonstrating that what you're selling is a good deal, or by convincing them that they might even be making some kind of investment! This latter strategy of course works particularly well when you're selling something like a make money online course!

Urgency and Scarcity

What is key to understand when selling, is that people buy based on their emotions and not logic. This is the reason that the whole 'value proposition' concept is so important: if you try and sell based on logic alone, then people will often realize they don't really need what you're offering and talk themselves out of it.

But if you convince them based on emotion, then they'll feel strongly compelled to buy and will find it hard to resist that temptation. The difference is huge and ultimately leads to a lot more sales.

This is also why it's often a good idea to try and get people to imagine owning your product and to make it seem desirable in its own right: in particular, this means using the right language: words like 'feel' and 'looks' help to really paint a picture and are often used by the likes of Steve Jobs and others when selling products.

The key is to get people to act on that emotion while it is there, rather than going away and coming back. To do this, you can introduce scarcity and urgency. That means pointing out that your audience needs to buy right now, or risk missing out entirely. You can do this by making out that you only have a very limited number of products left for sale, or by introducing a limited-time discount. Your readers will then conclude that if they are at all interested in what you're offering, they should buy right away rather than risk missing out on the opportunity. That way, they'll act on their emotional impulse, rather than leaving and deciding against it!

Chapter 5: Adding Polish and Mixing it Up – The Bit Everyone Forgets

If you tick all these boxes, then you will have a sales funnel that will be effective in capturing visitors and converting them into customers. You're grabbing their details every time they interact with your brand and then you're building their trust and growing your authority.

But is this alone enough to guarantee your success?

Unfortunately, there's just one big thing that is missing here – and that's making sure that all of the materials you've created are *good*.

Take a look around Facebook and you will see plenty of adverts for make-money-online schemes and for fitness programs. If you click them, you'll be taken straight to a sales funnel that will work just like the ones we've outlined in these pages.

But very often, you will find they really don't work on you.

Why? Because they look like spam.

We've all seen a thousand make-money-online sales funnels. We've all been to sales pages with people on yachts or beaches telling us how we can earn money from home and live the dream. The problem is, we just don't believe it any more!

And why should we? Often these sites look like they were made by a 15 year old, the promises are over the top and it's something we've seen 100 times before. And then there's the question we always ask ourselves in these situations: if this person is so rich, why does their website look so cheap?

And why are they doing this at all?

Hmmmm.

So you need to avoid this. And the way you're going to do that is by giving your funnel polish and by doing what you can to stand out. This means building a proper brand and it means investing in your funnel – hiring experts to help you with your design and with your video creation.

Imagine how much different the exact same strategy would be but where the first stage of your funnel was a professional edited video with premium production values. That means a high quality camera, quality editing, a good script, music and more.

This inspires so much more trust in your brand instantly and makes you stand out from tons of second rate spammers on the web. The same goes for offering something a bit different and for thinking of new and unique ways to engage with your audience.

Never forget to actually build value – don't just *appear* to be offering it!

Chapter 6: Pricing Strategy for Your Sales Funnel

The next important thing you need to think about is how you're going to price your funnel.

We know already that your first few touches are going to be 'free' and we've discussed in detail the value of charging for something smaller before you try and sell your 'big ticket' item. This also has the advantage of meaning that even people who will never be willing to pay for the big ticket item will *still* be able to spend some money with you and become paying customers.

But now we're going to look at pricing in a little more detail, because it's an important consideration. Once again, there are steps and rungs and you're going to be increasing the 'cost' of what you offer very slowly as you go.

The Free Line

The first step of course is completely free. This is your YouTube video or your blog – it's something that people can consume completely for free and then just leave without any kind of commitment.

The 'free line' is often the term used to describe the cut-off point where your content and your value *stops* being free. And often, this is shown in diagrams to be the entry point of the funnel. As they enter the funnel, they commit to start paying.

Things that go above the free line might include:

- Blogging
- Guest blogging
- Ezines
- Ebooks
- Press releases
- Free reports
- Camtasias
- Seminars
- Presentations

Having a 'free line' and knowing where precisely your free line sits can help you a great deal to manage your business and to test what is working well for you.

What's interesting is that more and more marketers are now talking about 'moving the free line'. Specifically, they are discussing moving the free line down and making more of the things they *used* to charge for free. This is a great way to get more people to commit to the funnel and to get ahead of the competition. Many people even recommend that you give away your very best stuff – the company that provides the most value *above the free line* is often the company that wins!

Collecting Details

While it's possible to think about your business like this, what you should also recognize is that details are not *"free"*. This is an important thing to understand because while a visitor isn't 'paying' you when they sign up for your mailing list, there is still a cost to them, that being their information. This is still a transaction and you still need to be able to offer something worthwhile to them in exchange for those details.

What's more is that this moves them inexorably toward buying from you. Once they've made the step of handing over their details, they have already made one kind of 'payment' in a sense. Now it is going to seem like a smaller step for them to move toward making a small purchase, especially once they've made that commitment.

Choosing Prices

Now you know where your free line is and you recognize that it is moveable by nature, the next thing to consider is the *precise* price you're going to set for the items that are *below* the free line.

This is important because this is still part of your puzzle. We've talked about selling one smaller item to get people ready to pay for more expensive items. Very often your sales funnel will go further than this and will involve multiple purchases, each getting more and more expensive.

But at each step of the way, you still need to ensure you are providing value and offering something in exchange for what you're charging that is worth that amount.

How do you work out what your products and services are worth? There are a few options...

1. Do your market research. Look at what other brands and companies are charging for the equivalent products and offer the same.

2. Look at the ways products similar to yours are calculated. For instance, if you are selling items you purchased wholesale, then you might well use the typical 'keystone pricing' approach. This means that you are going to charge your end customer twice the amount that you paid for the product, thereby making a 100% profit.

3. You'll also need to calculate your COGS. COGS is 'Cost Of Goods Sold' and tells you how much each item you are selling cost you to manufacture. Working this out tells you how much you need to charge in order to make a profit. You can then think about the amount you're going to *need* to grow and scale your business, while also maintaining a healthy lifestyle.

4. This doesn't work with e-books because you don't have any overheads. The cost of manufacturing an e-book is nil! So how can you be sure you're offering the right value for money? Simple – you test the market and see what your e-book will sell for. Look at similar products, and then try tweaking your price to see if your overall profits increase or decrease.

5. Read your metrics. As you get more advanced, the only real option is to closely watch your metrics and see what is working. This means, for example, identifying how much a customer is *worth* to you once they reach the 5th rung. Because what you might find is that it's actually worth selling the first item in your sales funnel at a loss, if it means that you can subsequently increase the chances of selling your last item. The only way to know this for sure though, is to

carefully monitor your sales and see who is buying what and how much it is earning you at each point in the funnel.

Contrast, Discounts and More

Finally, remember that you need to leave a little 'wiggle room' in your price. If you're going to make a big sale quickly, we've already discussed that you will want to increase urgency and scarcity. One way to do this is by offering a limited-time discount, but that means you need to make the product expensive enough that you can offer said discount and still be making a profit!

And if you're selling multiple products, then there are various different ways that the costs can interact that you also need to take on board. For instance, when you are selling more than one item you might use a strategy called 'contrast'. This means that you're placing a cheaper item next to a more expensive item. This makes the more expensive item appear more premium and it again introduces that idea of increasing the price in small intervals. A customer might convince themselves to spend $10 more as that's a small price to pay to get the *very best* (as they were buying already anyway).

Conversely, if the customer wants to be frugal, then they might buy the cheaper item because it will *appear* like a better deal when next to the more expensive option. They can thus overcome their buyers' remorse by saying to themselves: 'okay, well then, I'll *just get the cheaper item*'.

Chapter 7: Playing the Long Game and Building Trust

What's crucial to consider throughout all of this, is that you are building trust and playing the long game. Remember, we're aiming to do the precise *opposite* of that guy in the street offering watches. We know that we need to woo our customers and get them 'on side' before we try and sell them something worth thousands of dollars. It seems obvious but it's crazy how many people will never think of it this way!

The next question is precisely how you're going to build that trust. How *do* you generate 'true fans' and how do you make sure that the experience at each stage of your funnel is a worthwhile one?

The first tip of course is just to make your products *good* and that goes for your free ones above the line too. I have worked with clients that create sales funnels where the first product is a folder filled with six silent videos of people setting up WordPress. And they call this 'The Ultimate Guide to Generating Online Income' or something of the sort. What chance do you think that person has of selling something for $1,000?

Over delivering

The concept we need to discuss here is over delivering. Instead of creating something that falls sadly short, you need to make sure that your products and experiences are *over delivering* each time. That means that you are exceeding expectations and going above and beyond. If you promise an amazing e-book, then throw in extra videos, extra mind maps and beautiful big images. Surpass expectations and you'll create good will that will spur extra sales!

This is why the best sellers on Amazon never promise next day delivery. They promise delivery in 2-4 days and then make sure it arrives the next day. Customers are almost always blown away by this and that means positive reviews and more sales!

Your Mission Statement

The other way to make sure that people want to be your fan and that they actually get behind your brand is to *have a brand*. 'EasyCashOnline' is not a brand – it's a keyword. Moreover, a good brand goes beyond just a name and a logo.

A brand should *begin* with a promise, with a call to action and with a 'mission statement'. The best companies – the ones that really inspire people and that create big movements – those are the ones that have some kind of vision for themselves and for the world. Apple was so successful in its heyday because it was all about disrupting the establishment and making computers that were fun and friendly to use – it was about taking that power out of the hands of the elite and giving it to the masses. This was a vision and a passion and it took over the world.

And you see this with all the most successful brands in the world. They have an identifier, a unifying cause, morals and a vision. Try to work out what it was that inspired you to get into business, try and work out where you want to *go* with your business and what you want to give back. Now put all of that into a 'mission statement' and make sure you refer to that with every decision you make, with every piece of branding and with every piece of marketing. When you do, you will create something that people can get behind and that excites people.

This is the kind of thing that people become 'true fans' of and it's what will encourage people to want to become more and more committed to your brand as they keep reading.

Content Marketing

This all ties in perfectly with content marketing. Content marketing simply means that you're relying on the free content you post on your blog (and possibly guest post on other blogs) in order to reach your audience. You'll use this content to build up your SEO and to share on social media but at the same time, it's also going to provide that vital first touch and provide value to the user while building trust.

There are plenty of different options when it comes to digital marketing but the one that will *always* work best with a sales funnel is content marketing.

Chapter 8: Crucial Tools and Resources That Will Save You Time

Building Your Sales/Squeeze Pages

As mentioned in an earlier chapter, one of the most important things that can help you to increase your sales and your conversions is to create a great sales page with the right persuasive language.

But your persuasive language is only one piece of that puzzle. What's equally important is that you have a well-designed page that will encourage people to want to buy from you and that will keep them engaged. A great way to do this is with the right WordPress theme or plugin and one of the very best to this end is 'Optimize Press' for WordPress.

Optimize Press will instantly turn any site into a sales page, using the standard long, narrow design and a lack of buttons leading away from your sales page. The design has been built with a lot of testing and has been shown to maximize conversion rates and this way you aren't relying on your own design skills or trial and error. Let the pros take care of the design and you just focus on the write-up! You can find Optimize Press at www.optimizepress.com.

Another tool is called ClickFunnels (https://clickfunnels.com). ClickFunnels make is quick and easy to setup landing pages as well as backend sales pages such as upsells and downsells.

An essential service to use is PayPal. This is the most popular way to accept transactions and can be used in a multiple number of ways, the simplest being just to embed the 'Pay Now' button your site and then send out the digital products manually. PayPal is well recognized and lots of people already have an account, which reduces the barrier to sale by ensuring people don't need to enter their details into an unknown form.

Webinars and Meetings

A staple of good sales funnels is to host webinars and online presentations. There are a number of different things you can use to do this and a number of different tools for creating great online webinars.

Some of the best include GoToMeeting/GoToWebinar, U-Conference, Google Hangouts, Webinarjam and Easy Webinar Plugin.

But why not try live streaming as mentioned? Periscope, Facebook Live and Meerkat all offer this option.

Google Analytics

For metrics, the most important thing to set up is Google Analytics and 'Goal Tracking'. Goal tracking allows you to look at precisely who is making it to your checkout page and your 'thank you for buying page' using cookies. You can then see how those visitors behaved prior to buying and you can see which searches led to that action etc. This is invaluable data to use for fine tuning your funnel, which we'll be looking at in the next chapter.

Lead Management

Another thing to consider is how you will manage your leads. This is going to mean creating a mailing list for most people and then using an autoresponder in order to manage those emails. Your autoresponder is basically the tool that you'll use to collect your emails (via a form you'll build to put on your site) as well as to send them out. You can then log in to the autoresponder and create your emails, before clicking once to deliver them to everyone on that list.

Autoresponders also perform a range of other jobs, for example they will let you manage unsubscribes and create a 'double opt-in' process, meaning that users need to confirm their email addresses (thereby avoiding people signing up with fake emails and helping you to ensure all your subscribers really are going to read your messages).

Perhaps one of the most powerful features of many autoresponders though, is the option to see how engaged your various readers are. You'll be able to see for example how many people are opening each email and which of your users really aren't engaging at all. More usefully, you'll be able to identify the people who always open emails and who always click on the links. These are your more engaged users and your more qualified leads. In other words, they're the ones who are ready to move on to the next stage in your funnel and you can set up your autoresponder to email them only once they reach this certain point.

Lead Scoring

We've mentioned leads a few times in this book so far. Of course a lead is anyone who you can potentially sell too but they will vary in terms of how useful they are and *how* likely they are to be willing to buy.

A cold lead is someone who has never heard of you before. This is the person who has just landed on your site or who is seeing an ad from you for the first time. A warm lead is someone who has shown some kind of interest by subscribing, liking you on social media etc. Your qualified lead is someone who has shown interest in a product by getting a quote or by spending time in your store. This is the person who is the easiest to now convert into a customer.

Your job of course is to take your visitors from cold leads all the way to qualified leads. And one way to make this easier is by lead scoring – calculating just *how* warm each lead is and how far away they are from being qualified. The best autoresponder software will do this for you and make it much easier to message the right people at the right time – because timing is everything when it comes to sales!

Some of the best autoresponders on the market are:

- Aweber (http://aweber.com)
- GetResponse (http://www.getresponse.com)
- MailChimp (www.mailchimp.com)

Ultimately, all three of these tools are very similar in terms of the features and services they provide, so what's left is to consider the pricing and which best suits your targets.

Chapter 9: Increasing Conversion Rates

Once your sales funnel is set up and live, all that's left to do is to watch as the sales come in and then tweak it to try and generate more revenue and more profit.

The best way to do this is to increase your conversion rates at each stage of the funnel. How do you make sure that more people go from visiting your site to signing up for your mailing list? And how do you encourage them to go from buying your cheapest item, to buying your most expensive item?

Investment

One simple answer is to invest. We discussed this already when we talked about adding polish – but it's something you can *continue* to do with time. As money starts to come in from your sales, invest that *back* into your funnel by improving each step of the process. That means making your products better by adding more sheen and more freebies, it means making your videos better, it means investing in more marketing (see below) and it means building a better brand with the right logo and the right web design.

Hire writers, hire web designers and generally keep growing and improving your business. Your job is not 'done' once it goes live!

PPC

One of the easiest ways to increase your conversion rates is to improve your targeting. And one of the best ways to get more targeted visitors to your sites, other than using your established 'routes to market', is to use PPC to create targeted adverts.

PPC is 'Pay Per Click' advertising and is most commonly associated with either Google AdWords or Facebook Ads. Both types of advertising allow very precise targeting for your campaigns so that you can ensure your ads are being seen by the right people. For example, on Facebook, you can choose adverts that are only seen by people with certain hobbies listed, people in certain locations or people with certain jobs.

Likewise, on Google AdWords, you can target people based on the searches they perform. Adverts on Google AdWords appear on the SERPs – Search Engine Results Pages. This means that you can place your ads for watches on the search 'Buy Watches Online'. It's safe to assume that people searching that term will have an interest in buying watches!

The other great thing about PPC is that you can set your 'CPC' – Cost Per Click. This means you choose a maximum amount that you're willing to pay for each visitor who clicks your ad and visits your site. The more you pay, the more your ad will be seen – but if you choose the right keywords then you can get visitors for a surprisingly small amount of money.

Now, if you can work out how many of your visitors eventually become paying customers and you can work out how much each of those sales means for you in profits, then you can calculate the amount that you can pay for each visitor and still be guaranteed a profit! This is the step *before* your sales funnel – and it's equally as important.

Watching Metrics

Also very important is to look at your reports and metrics. Track which adverts are bringing customers to you site, look at which products are selling best and even look at what times of day are the most active for you. Most importantly – look at where your best customers are coming from. This is important because you can then invest more time and more money into what is working and start to move *away* from what isn't working. This is where Google Analytics and Goal Tracking come in particularly useful.

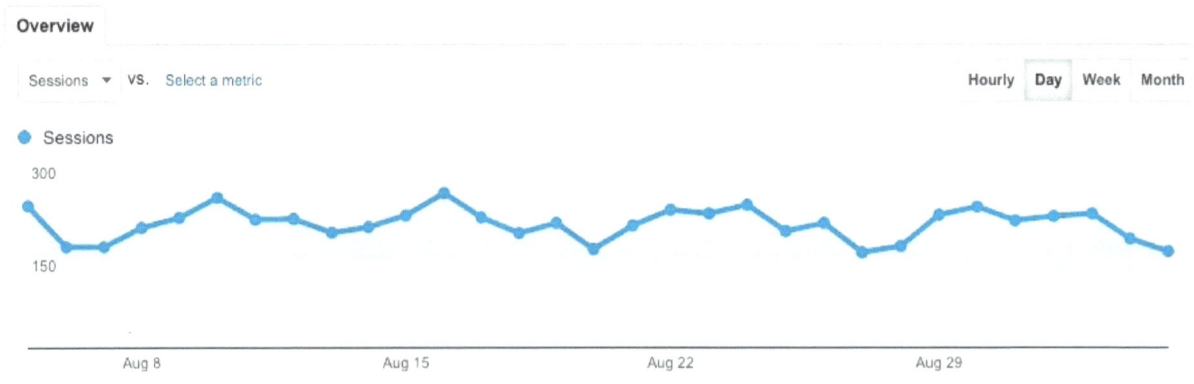

Another way you can do this is by using split testing. Split testing means creating two versions of a web page (such as your squeeze page) and then introducing subtle differences to each version. You then see which of your two versions performs best and therefore decide whether or not to keep or abandon those changes. There are tools that let you do this, such as Optimizely.

Building True Fans

Finally, try to think of your objectives in terms of building true fans. One of the most important things you can do is to really get people behind your business and to feel almost as though they know you and as though they're a friend. When you have a true fan, they will not only be most likely to buy from you but they will also be likely to share your content, spread the word and help you grow your business.

This is why it *is* worthwhile spending time in one-on-one chats, in answering emails and comments and in generally engaging with your audience. Meanwhile, don't think about them in terms of how you can sell to them – just think about how you can provide value and provide a good, free service. Some of these people will never buy from you but that's not the point. The ones that do will make all that hard work worthwhile. If you create something really good and deliver a really great service, then you'll be rewarded.

A great article about "true fans" is an article by Kevin Kelly. He has a theory about '1000 true fans'. Read it here:

http://kk.org/thetechnium/1000-true-fans/

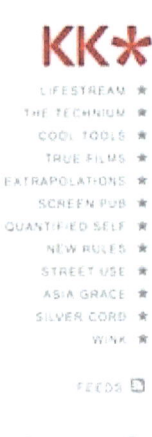

LIFESTREAM ★
THE TECHNIUM ★
COOL TOOLS ★
TRUE FILMS ★
EXTRAPOLATIONS ★
SCREEN PUB ★
QUANTIFIED SELF ★
NEW RULES ★
STREET USE ★
ASIA GRACE ★
SILVER CORD ★
WINK ★

FEEDS

Search

Most Popular Postings

1,000 True Fans
I'll Pay You to Read My Book
The Shirky Principle
The Post-Productive Economy
Better Than Free

ARCHIVES

The Wikipedia Deletion Wars
Non-Commodificable in Newsprint
BIL, the Unconference
Evolution and Ontogeny of Game Characters
The Near-Death Experience of Dying in a Game
The Variety of Polyhedrons
The Kitchen Computer
Flash Presentations, 20/20
Live HD
Work Habits
Circle of Life
Subterranean Tutoring
The Bottom is Not Enough
An Eternal Last Goodbye
Defining Waterboarding
Freeconomy
Visual Music Instruments
Downtailing
Playing Digital Games Together
Better Than Free
Forest-Fire Marketing
Incremental vs. Discrete Content
The Platform is the Computer
How Buildings Learn
Social Networking Chain-Letter
Election Prediction Markets
The Future Doesn't Matter
Lumpers and Splitters
Doomsday Art
Sanctuaries of Disconnection
How Not to Do a Time Capsule
Addiction Vaccines
Believing the Impossible
Videogame Symphonies
Computational Advertising
How To Find a Doctor
Extra-less Films
International Burning Man, 2008
My Dream Machine
The iPhone Interface of the Future
The Future is Not Vending Machines

THE TECHNIUM

1,000 True Fans
< previous   next >

[Translations: Chinese, French, German, Hebrew, Italian, Japanese, Portuguese, Romanian, Spanish]

The long tail is famously good news for two classes of people; a few lucky aggregators, such as Amazon and Netflix, and 6 billion consumers. Of those two, I think consumers earn the greater reward from the wealth hidden in infinite niches.

But the long tail is a decidedly mixed blessing for creators. Individual artists, producers, inventors and makers are overlooked in the equation. The long tail does not raise the sales of creators much, but it does add massive competition and endless downward pressure on prices. Unless artists become a large aggregator of other artist's works, the long tail offers no path out of the quiet doldrums of minuscule sales.

Other than aim for a blockbuster hit, what can an artist do to escape the long tail?

One solution is to find 1,000 True Fans. While some artists have discovered this path without calling it that, I think it is worth trying to formalize. The gist of 1,000 True Fans can be stated simply:

A creator, such as an artist, musician, photographer, craftsperson, performer, animator, designer, videomaker, or author – in other words, anyone producing works of art – needs to acquire only 1,000 True Fans to make a living.

A True Fan is defined as someone who will purchase anything and everything you produce. They will drive 200 miles to see you sing. They will buy the super deluxe re-issued hi-res box set of your stuff even though they have the low-res version. They have a Google Alert set for your name. They bookmark the eBay page where your out-of-print editions show up. They come to your openings. They have you sign their copies. They buy the t-shirt, and the mug, and the hat. They can't wait till you issue your next work. They are true fans.

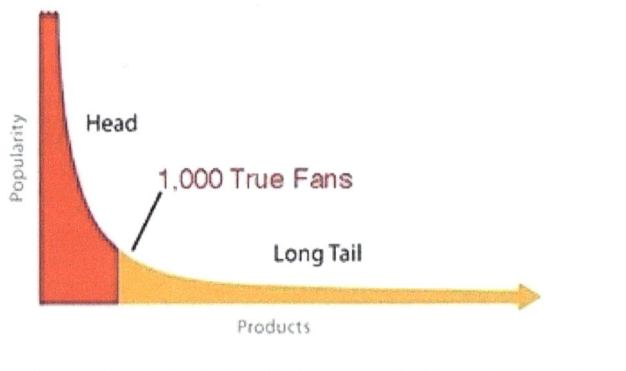

To raise your sales out of the flatline of the long tail you need to connect with your True Fans

Chapter 10: Choosing Your Products

Finally, you need to make sure that you have chosen the right products to begin with. This might seem obvious but the product you choose will not only impact on your sales but also on the type of customer you get, the type of marketing you use and even the subject you write about.

So how do you go about choosing the right products?

A good place to start is by thinking about what you want to write about and what resources you already have available to you. If you happen to run the world's most popular fitness site, then you should probably develop (or buy) a fitness product! If you don't own a website though, you might still decide that fitness is a subject you'd be happy to write about and this is very important if you're going to stay committed to the process of writing every single day! Likewise, you need to know about your niche if you're really going to offer good value in your blog posts and your reports.

Another pointer is to consider any routes to market you might *already* have. Do you just so happen to know the editor of a magazine with a huge circulation? Do you happen to know a big YouTuber? If you already have access to a specific personal, all that is left to do is to craft your funnel for that personal.

Then think about how easy the product will be to sell. What is the competition like? Is the market saturated? Does the product have a value proposition that people won't be able to ignore? Selling people great abs or a better love life is always going to lead to more profit than a book on sewing…

Finally, it's always a good idea to test out your idea before you invest too much money in developing or marketing it. This is called 'validating' your product and you can do that by checking that other businesses have been able to sell it, or better yet, building up some interest and some pre-orders *before* you've even started building it!

Acquiring Products to Sell: Your Options

Once you know what you want to sell, there's just one more small issue… making it! Here's how you can go about making *or* acquiring a product to sell easily.

Creating Digital Products

The easiest products to make are digital products. You can easily make an e-book, an online course or a video series yourself or hire someone to do it for you through sites like UpWork (www.upwork.com).

Creating Physical Products

You can also create your own *physical* products! This is much harder of course though and might mean trying to find a manufacturer and coming up with plans.

Selling Affiliate Products

Whether you sell digital products or physical ones, you might decide it's easier to sell products other people created. This way, you are acting as a sales-person and keeping commission. It's harder to find truly big ticket items and you do lose some of the profit, but it can also save you a lot of time and completely remove any risk. It might be a good way to validate your sales funnel before investing in your own product creation. Find digital products on sites like JVZoo (www.jvzoo.com) and Commission Junction (www.cj.com) or physical ones on Amazon (www.amazon.com).

Drop shipping

Drop shipping is living the dream! This means selling someone else's product but with your name on it and with no need to mention the manufacturer. This is a white label service and you can find companies offering this on sites like Alibaba (www.ali baba.com).

Conclusion and Summary

And with that, you should now have all the information you need to start building your own sales funnel. We've looked at a lot of high concept ideas here and discussed the psychology of your buyers and how you can work that to your advantage. But remember, at the end of the day you still need a great brand, a great purpose and some excellent products; if you're going to inspire your audience and make some big sales. So try not to be cynical about this – start with a real vision but then just realize that you need to build a relationship and you need to build trust before you can sell your most expensive items.

To recap, the best ways to do this are to:

- Come up with a strong brand and a 'value proposition'

- Create a blog and use content marketing to build a following – or use a YouTube channel etc

- Drive cold leads with targeted PPC and other methods

- Encourage people to sign up for your mailing list

- Run a free webinar or conference to engage with your audience and make 'fans'

- Start moving people past your 'free line' by charging for smaller products

- Build trust and engagement and increase the price until you're able to ship your 'big ticket item'

- Use a sales page with well written persuasive writing to increase conversions

  - Your sale should amount to five 'touches' minimum
  - You should employ the AIDA technique to build interest and awareness

- Monitor and manage your funnel to gradually increase your sales further and improve conversion rates

Structure all this around a well-thought out product and spend time really building trust with your visitors. If you do this well, then you'll have the perfect strategy for attracting visitors and turning them into the kinds of loyal customers that will want to buy the big ticket items from you!

IMPORTANT: To help you further take action, print out a copy of the *Checklist* and *Mind map* I provided for you. You'll also find a Resource Cheat Sheet with valuable sites, posts and articles that I recommend you go through. If you purchased this book via kindle, you can visit www.tomkustra.com/sales-funnel-growth/bonus